D0297753

THE LIFE & TIMES OF

Julius Caesar

BY
A Noble

This edition first published by Parragon Books

Produced by
Magpie Books Ltd
7 Kensington Church Court
London W8 4SP

Cover picture & illustrations courtesy of: Mary Evans
Picture Library; Christies Images.

ISBN 1 85813 937 6

A copy of the British Library Cataloguing in Publication
Data is available from the British Library.

Typeset by Hewer Text Composition Services, Edinburgh
Printed in Singapore by Printlink International Co.

Gaius Julius Caesar, a member of the Julian family, was probably born in 100 BC, though some sources say he was born two years earlier. Very little is known of his childhood and events in his life are only reported when he reaches his late teens.

We do know, however, that he was born into a time of strife. Rome had been in a constitutional crisis for almost two hundred years, and this had come to a head a generation before Caesar. The crisis was ultimately due to the rapid expansion of the Roman state, as it took over the Italian peninsula and fought wars abroad, notably that with Carthage.

The image we have of the Roman Empire is one of stability and power. But the institutions that made it so did not exist before Caesar's time. To understand Caesar, we need to understand the world into which he was born.

ROME IN CRISIS

Originally, government positions in Rome – consuls, praetors, tribunes, etc. – were elective, to be held for one year. This short term of office prevented the holders from accumulating too much power – holders of offices could not be re-elected the following year. Also, by ensuring that several of the major patrician (aristocratic) families held offices in turn, it damped down internal rivalries. The only exception to these rules was in times of extreme crisis when the *imperium* would be granted to an individual; the *imperium* meant absolute power and the person so endowed was known as the dictator, effectively the one whose word was law. Governors also held the *imperium* in their provinces.

Rome had been ruled by an Assembly, where all citizens could vote, in which the main posts were those of consul and tribune. Two consuls were elected and ten tribunes. The consuls shared ceremonial duties and command of the army, even commanding the army on alternate days in some cases. The tribunes had to come from the *plebs* and had the right to propose and veto new laws in the Assembly, but had no other responsibilities. The route to consul was via quaestor, with financial responsibilities, aedile, responsible for public works and games, and praetor, whose role was to act as a judge. Consuls were judges and had administrative and religious duties. Consuls and praetors were also expected to assume the senior military commands in time of war – and Rome was at war somewhere or other for almost all of its 1,000-year history.

All the preceding roles came under the general heading of magistrate, which then had the broader meaning of office-holder. All magistrates automatically became members of the Senate. The role of the Senate was to debate proposed laws and actions on behalf of the Republic. In time, the ascendancy of the Senate over the Assembly became complete. Its edicts became law and it started to issue commands under the slogan 'SPQR' – *Senatus Populusque Romanus* the Senate and People of Rome.

All this started to change as Rome expanded both in Italy and overseas. New posts were created to rule in the provinces and colonies – proconsuls and propraetors. (The distinction between a province and a colony was that provinces were not settled by Roman farmers – ex-soldiers – whereas colonies were). Because of the difficulties of travel – either on foot or slowly by sea, with journeys to colonies often taking several months – it became impractical for proconsuls and propraetors to hold office for only one year. Once the one-year rule was broken, the consequences were predictable. Proconsuls and propraetors began to attract loyalty to themselves rather than to the Roman Republic. This was especially dangerous as one of their tasks was to raise armies to control and/or expand their governorships. These armies were loyal first to their leaders, then to the Republic.

In Rome itself, the electoral system was utterly corrupt. Candidates required huge sums of money, both for putting on spectacular games to win over the population, and to directly buy votes as they progressed up the political ladder. This meant that many senators went deeper and deeper into debt. The only means of paying back such debts was to conquer new territory and seize booty in enormous quantities. This meant that, ideally, one had to get oneself appointed as a proconsul or propraetor and raise an army. As there were too few positions to go round, there were always frustrated senators and tribunes hugely in debt, and thus ready to resort to desperate measures, including *coup d'états*.

The army had originally been a citizen army, essentially a militia, and this had been adequate when Rome was fighting to achieve dominance in Italy, where distances and campaigns were relatively short. Once, however, long campaigns began to be conducted at greater and greater distances from Rome, it changed in character and became professional, with soldiers serving long periods (up to twenty-five years), at the end of which they expected to be settled on land to farm, and during which they hoped to gain the spoils of battle. Marius was the first consul, towards the end of the second century BC, to recruit volunteers rather than conscripts. Unlike the militia who only wanted to return to their farms, these professional soldiers were loath to be disbanded at the end of wars and lose the prospect of plunder. This meant large standing-armies came into being.

And if they owed loyalty to rival generals, then the consequences were obvious.

Rome also suffered from having an enormous mob (some 320,000 by Caesar's time), paid for by the city with grants of free corn. Its existence had been caused by the dispossession of smallholders throughout Italy by the ancient equivalent of agribusiness – landholders who had made their wealth through war and the extortionate tax-farming of provinces, and who had, by the same means, acquired large numbers of slaves who worked the land for free. These smallholders had flocked to Rome but there was no work for them there, as the urban economy was also slave-based.

All these fundamental flaws in the constitution and state of Rome came to a head with

Marius and Sulla. Marius was elected consul
an unprecedented five times between 105
and 101 BC, having already held the post in
107. The Cimbri and Teutoni, two powerful
German tribes, had already defeated three
Roman armies, and were threatening to
advance on Rome. Marius destroyed the
Cimbri at Aquae Sextae (Aix-en-Provence)
and the Tentoni Vercellae. He then disbanded his army, but the Senate did not
honour his promises of land to his men.
This naturally led to extreme disgruntle-
ment on his part, and he entered politics
on the side of the *Populares* (the People's
Party). On his re-election as consul in 101
BC, he introduced laws to ensure that his
veterans received land and also claimed
further colonies in northern Italy and Gaul
to settle them. He also enfranchised the
Italian population (many of his soldiers were

Italians rather than Romans), which theoretically diluted the power of the Roman populace. This last measure was not well received by the *Optimates* (the 'best' people's party), a conservative, aristocratic group. The *equites*, the 'knights' who comprised the rich merchant-class and who monopolized tax-farming and agribusiness, ceased to support the *Populares*. The Roman population did not like Marius's reforms either. The result in 99 BC was rioting, murder and general disorder, including the murder of a consular candidate. Marius was temporarily made dictator. He suppressed the rioting and then left for the East, realizing he had the support of none of the parties in Rome.

In 91 BC trouble flared up again with the murder of Livius Drusus, a tribune. Rome's Italian allies, disgusted at the increasingly

Julius Caesar

Roman foot soldiers

outrageous state of Roman politics, rebelled. Rome immediately offered full citizenship-rights to those states that abandoned the revolt, known as the Social War, and sent two consular armies against the others. The legates (seconds in command) were Marius and Sulla. When the rebellion was nearly extinguished, Sulla was given the task of subduing Pontus (a kingdom on the north coast of modern Turkey) where Mithridates VI, the king, had taken the opportunity to overrun Roman possessions and kill all the Roman tax-collectors there. Marius, though, wanted to take over from Sulla so that he could reap the benefits of conquering Pontus. With the help of P. Sulpicius Rufus, a corrupt tribune, Marius had a law passed appointing him to command the campaign. But Sulla was in an invulnerable position and refused to obey the Senate's order that he hand his army over. And Sulla's men, recruited under Marius's volunteer system, were loyal to their general, not Rome, and as keen as Sulla to plunder Pontus. Sulla marched on Rome and occupied it. Marius fled and his laws were repealed. Consular elections were held and L. Cornelius Cinna and Gnaeus Octavius were elected in 87 BC. Sulla did not fully trust Cinna, but nonetheless left Rome for the East.

Virtually as soon as Sulla was gone, Cinna contacted Marius, who raised an army of slaves and brigands and seized Ostia, the port of Rome, thereby cutting off its food supply. Octavius's soldiers deserted to Marius and Cinna, and these two then seized Rome. An orgy of terror then ensued as Marius's men went on the rampage and slaughtered their enemies. Marius and Cinna then declared themselves consuls for 86 BC. They reversed Sulla's legislation, confiscated his property and caused his family to flee to Greece. Marius then died, shortly into his seventh consulship.

Sulla meanwhile carried on his campaign against Mithridates, successfully concluding the war in 85 BC. He had reaped untold riches from the campaign: after paying himself and his soldiers, he still contributed 15,000 pounds of gold and 115,000 pounds of silver to the Roman treasury. He now announced that he would be returning to Rome, and landed unopposed at Brundisium (Brindisi) in early 83 BC. He was joined by many *optimates*, including M. Licinius Crassus and Gnaeus Pompeius – Pompey the Great. Sulla defeated Marius the Younger, Marius's son and the other Marian generals.

(Cinna had perished in a mutiny, trying to persuade an army to go to Greece to prevent Sulla returning to Italy.)

When Sulla retook Rome he began a systematic programme of exterminating his opponents by proscription, slaughtering several thousand senators, exconsuls and knights. He seized their property and distributed it among 120,000 of his soldiers. Some Italian states lost their Roman citizenship and others were ravaged as punishment. Sulla also formed a bodyguard from 10,000 freed slaves, a forerunner of the Praetorian Guard. He then had the Senate declare him dictator for life, effectively making himself king in all but name, thus paving the way for Julius Caesar and Augustus. Much of the system he left untouched, apart from making it impossible for consuls, praetors and tribunes to be re-elected within ten years of holding their posts. The governors of the provinces were also forbidden to leave their provinces or go to war without the approval of the Senate.

Julius Caesar was lucky to survive this period: his aunt had been married to Marius and he was a recognized member of the Marian party. It was only through the intercession of the Vestal Virgins that he survived.

THE 'GREAT' RIVAL

Sulla died in 78 BC, having resigned the dictatorship. Almost instantly, Rome subsided into chaos again. Q. Lutatius Catulus and M. Aemilius Lepidus were the consuls in 78 BC. Lepidus wanted to restore the fortunes of the Marian party. This encouraged the Italian states, and one, Etruria, which had lost Roman citizenship under Sulla, rebelled, throwing out those veterans of Sulla's army who had been settled there. The Senate ordered Lepidus to crush the rebellion, but instead he switched sides and marched his army on Rome. In desperation, the Senate called on Pompey to defend it.

In short order, Pompey took to the field and defeated Lepidus, but failed to stop him and his army escaping to Sardinia. Lepidus died shortly thereafter and his army then sailed to Spain under Vento Perpenna to join Sertorius, an able Marian general, who was in effective control of the province. Pompey left for Spain in late 77 BC, crossing the Pyrenees in early 76 BC. As with so many campaigns in Spain, it was a guerrilla war, and Pompey only really achieved victory in 72 BC with the assassination of Sertorius at the instigation of Perpenna.

Pompey's star glowed more brightly, though, with the Spartacus Revolt. Spartacus, a Thracian gladiator, had escaped with seventy comrades from gladiatorial school in Capua. He and his followers sheltered in the crater of Mount Vesuvius, where they were joined by many escaped slaves and other criminals. Soldiers were sent against them, but were defeated, which encouraged many malcontents to join the revolt. Spartacus eventually commanded 70,000 men. A consular army was defeated and the Senate had to call on Crassus, who was a praetor in 72 BC, to raise six new legions to destroy Spartacus's army. Crassus managed to hem Spartacus in the toe of Italy and then defeated him in Lucania. Pompey's army met up with fugitives from this battle and wiped them out. Crassus meanwhile crucified 6,000 captives along the Appian Way between Capua and Rome. This left two armies in Italy, Pompey's and Crassus's, but

Caesar was responsible for the public games

The luxuries of the imperial court

despite the personal dislike of the two men for each other, they did not want to fight a civil war. Crassus, an immensely rich man, had the support of the Senate, half of whom owed him money, and Pompey had the support of the people for his successes in the field. The two men camped their armies outside Rome until they were elected consuls. They successfully disbanded their armies, and proceeded to reverse the legislation of Sulla. Both men retired when their consulships terminated at the end of 70 BC.

Pompey then spent the next two years in private life before coming up with a plan that would restore his fortunes. Because of the chronic strife in Rome, piracy in the Mediterranean had become a major problem: pirates had banded together and had a fleet of 1,000, with headquarters in Crete and Cilicia (south-eastern Turkey). They were strong enough to attack coastal towns and kidnap locals for ransom. More importantly, they threatened the corn supply to Rome, which was transported from Sicily, Sardinia and the northern coast of Africa. Because shortages of corn had been the cause of much unrest in Rome, the pirates had become a major political issue. Pompey had a supporter propose in the Assembly that a dictator of the seas be appointed, to command 200 ships, with responsibility for the whole Mediterranean. This would have been the largest command ever held by a Roman general. The Senate opposed this, guessing correctly who expected to be the appointee, but the people forced Pompey's election. Pompey immediately proposed that the fleet be increased to 500 and that he receive an army of 120,000. This bill was carried and the price of grain fell. Pompey then set sail and, within three months, swept the pirates from the sea.

He finished his campaign in the eastern Mediterranean and then took over there from two ineffectual consuls who were struggling with Mithridates. Within two years, Pompey had taken Syria and Pontus and Jerusalem, and had effectively created a lasting eastern empire for the Romans. He returned to Italy in triumph at the end of 62 BC, having promised to generously reward his men with land and money. The Senate quaked at news of his approach, but Pompey disbanded his army. The Senate refused to ratify any of the grants of land that Pompey had made. Caesar would not repeat this mistake.

THE MANTLE
OF THE GODS

The family of Gaius Julius Caesar was an ancient one. It was patrician, and as such mostly supported the *optimates*, but Julius was a *popularis* due to his aunt Julia having married Marius. Caesar's tutor was M. Antonius Gnipho, a well-educated Gaul, who passed on his knowledge of Roman and Greek culture to his able student. Caesar's first post was that of *flamen dialis* (Priest of Jupiter), to which he was appointed by

Marius and Cinna in 84 BC. He also married Cinna's daughter Cornelia, to cement the families' political relationship.

On Sulla's return, Caesar was lucky to escape with his life. Sulla had ordered Pompey and Caesar to divorce their wives, but Caesar refused. Suetonius, writing 150 years later, but with access to contemporary records, has it that Sulla predicted that Caesar would be the ruin of the *optimates*, being much greater than Marius. Shortly after his near-fatal encounter with Sulla, Caesar obviously thought it wise to put some distance between himself and Rome. He joined the staff of Minucius Thermus, the praetor in Bithynia (north-western Turkey), in 81 BC. During this period, he received a civic crown for saving a soldier's life at the siege of Mitylene. He then moved to Cilicia for a brief period

under the consul Servilius Isauricus, returning to Italy only when he heard that Sulla
had died. He toyed with the idea of joining
Lepidus in his rebellion but wisely thought
better of it.

Back in Rome, Caesar decided to establish a
reputation as a jurist, and acted for the
prosecution in the case of C. Cornelius
Dolabella, laying a charge of extortion.
Although Dolabella was acquitted, Caesar's
eloquence gained him many admirers. To
polish his rhetorical skills, he left Italy in 75
BC for Rhodes to study under Apollonius
Molon. On his way there an incident oc-
curred that illustrates his character. He was
captured by pirates. They proposed a ransom
of twenty talents, which Caesar told them
was too small a sum – he was worth at least
fifty. He stayed with the pirates for six weeks,

A Roman provincial town

A Roman general's tunic

waiting for the ransom to arrive. During that period he bantered with them, saying that he would return and crucify them (the standard punishment for piracy) as soon as he was free. Once out of their hands, he hired some galleys with crews, returned, and captured the pirates, regaining his ransom and other booty besides. He then kept his word and crucified his prisoners; not being vindictive, he had their throats cut so that they would not suffer a lingering death.

Little is known of the next few years. He was involved in the Third Mithridatic War with some success, being elected a military tribune on his return to Rome – the first example of public recognition in his life. In 69 BC he was elected quaestor, and in 68 BC he was on the staff of C. Antistius Vetus, praetor of Further Spain. While in Spain, at Gades (Cadiz), he saw a statue of Alexander the Great; reflecting on his comparatively slow progress, he decided to return to Rome to seek greater opportunities. *En route*, he took up the cause of the Transpadane Gauls, who were seeking full Roman citizenship. When back in Rome, he married Pompeia, Sulla's granddaughter. She was a rich heiress and this was a great inducement to an aspiring politician; also, it may have indicated that Caesar wished to conciliate the *optimates*.

Crassus now sought out the political aid of Caesar; although he was immensely rich, he was not particularly popular. Caesar was quite popular because he had supported Pompey in his eastern ventures, but needed money to pay for the games he would have to put on if he were to become an aedile. In 66 BC, Crassus was elected censor; and Caesar, aedile. Caesar then proceeded to put on spectacular games, surpassing in scale and expense any that had gone before, presumably using Crassus's money. The result was a great increase in his popularity. Crassus meanwhile proposed granting the Transpadane Gauls their citizenship. This was opposed, but Crassus knew it would make allies for him of the Transpadanes. He also proposed the annexation of Egypt, which usually had a large corn surplus. It would have given Caesar a reasonable pretext for raising an army. But, since Pompey had secured grain supplies by defeating the pirates, there was little interest in this project, and the knights had enough to plunder in the new provinces he had added in the east.

Crassus and Caesar then attempted to revive the scheme by getting two of their supporters, Catiline and Caius Antonius, elected consuls in 65 BC. Catiline had led a conspiracy to murder the consuls of 66 BC; he had only been absolved by the Senate on Crassus's intervention. Catiline was violently opposed by Cicero, who was elected instead with Antonius. This virtually put an end to the scheme: Cicero was adamantly against it and able to persuade the Senate to reject it in whatever guise it was presented. But Caesar was elected Pontifex Maximus, a life position.

The consular elections for 62 BC were held in October 63 BC. Catiline was now desperate to be elected consul as he had run up spectacular debts; if he was not elected, he would attempt a *coup d'état*. He hoped to call upon others in a similar situation to his own. When he was again not elected, he immediately put his plan into action. His colleague Gaius Manlius was to lead a revolt in Etruria, where most of Sulla's men had settled, and P. Cornelius Lentulus was to seize Rome. Cicero heard of the scheme from the mistress of one of the conspirators – and from Crassus and Caesar, who were eager to distance themselves from the conspirators – and convened the Senate, which granted him the power to raise an army to defeat the rebels. Manlius rebelled, Catiline fled to join him in Etruria, and the slaves in Capua and Apulia revolted. Lentulus was arrested. Caesar then argued clemency for the rebels but was opposed by Cato, who won the support of the Senate. Cicero had Lentulus and his accomplices strangled without trial. News of their deaths disheartened the rebels and Manlius's army shrank from 12,000 to 3,000. It was cornered and destroyed by

Cicero, and Catiline's head was sent back to Rome for display.

Caesar became praetor in 62 BC, and was appointed propraetor of Further Spain at the end of his praetorship. This was his first independent military command, and he made the most of it. In summer 61 BC he set off, after Crassus had settled most of his debts (25 million sesterces). Immediately he took the field, suppressing the local tribes in Lusitania (Portugal), and sending the booty back to Rome. At the end of his propraetorship he went back to Rome to seek a consulship. His popularity was almost bound to ensure his election. To become consul, Caesar had to enter Rome; but to receive a triumph (a celebratory parade to mark military successes), a general had to remain outside Rome until granted the right to retain his *imperium* within the city. The Senate, rather than viewing Caesar as a counterbalance to Pompey, rejected his request for permission to enter the consular race by registering by proxy. The Senate also made sure that M. Calpurnius Bibulus was elected – he was an enemy of Caesar – and converted the Civil Department of Forests and Cattle Drifts into a joint consular province, thereby depriving Caesar of the normal consular income.

Caesar immediately began talks with the disgruntled Pompey, whose men had not received the land he had promised them because of the hostility of the Senate. Caesar co-opted Crassus, and the first triumvirate came into being. Crassus had money; Caesar, popularity; and Pompey, soldiers – a potent combination. Caesar then proposed a bill to ensure that Pompey's men received their promised reward: in the Senate, Cato began to obstruct the bill. Caesar had him dragged out of the Senate; but when other senators followed, he adjourned the Senate and put the measure to the people. He knew he had popular support and Pompey had secretly arranged for some of his veterans to be present at the Assembly in the Forum. Crassus and Pompey spoke for the bill, but the tribunes vetoed it. In the ensuring uproar, Pompey's soldiers cleared the opposition from the Forum, a bucket of dung was poured over Bibulus, and the bill was passed. The Senate was completely wrongfooted by the triumvirate, whose existence it had been unaware of, and they could not get Bibulus to crush it as he had no soldiers.

Caesar now prepared for the next stage of his career, the acquisition of a province. Through his placemen, he was allotted Cisalpine Gaul and Illyricum (Yugoslavia). By a stroke of good fortune, the new governor of Transalpine Gaul died and Caesar was granted this governorship as well. Because of his control of the Senate, he ensured too that his proconsulship was for five years instead of the usual two. Before leaving, he dealt with his opponents: it was made a retrospective crime to execute suspects without trial, as Cicero had done with Lentulus. Cicero fled into exile. To deal with Cato and other senatorial opposition, Caesar ensured that Publius Clodius, an odious and ruthless patrician was appointed a tribune.

Caesar now heard that the Helvetii (a Swiss

tribe) were about to migrate into Gaul. With Titus Labienus, he raced off to Geneva. Fortune beckoned and Caesar answered her call.

Caesar crosses the Rubicon

A Roman centurion's helmet

GALLIC VICTORY

Gaul in Caesar's time extended from the Province (Provence) to the North Sea, including parts of modern Switzerland, Belgium and Holland. It was populated by Celtic tribes, from two to three hundred of them, and was considered quite a rich area at the time. It was semi-civilized, farming and trading with many other lands. Central control by chiefs was not very efficient, as every village had its own interests. The only unifying factor was the

Druids, who elected a Chief Druid for life.
The Druids met once a year, when they
would often adjudicate on tribal disputes.
The nobles spent much of their time attack-
ing other tribes.

The Germans were much tougher: they
despised the agricultural life, considering it
too peaceful and sedentary. They preferred
hunting and war. They considered raiding
and plundering as healthy exercise. They
were also excellent horsemen, which gave
them great mobility for surprise attacks,
though they often fought on foot.

The Helvetii, a people numbering some
368,000, including 92,000 warriors, according to Caesar, wanted to leave western
Switzerland as they were worried about
the presence of Ariovistus, a successful Ger-

man war-lord, who had established himself in Gaul by defeating several Gallic tribes. They wanted to move to western Gaul, to an area bordering that of the Tolosates (who lived round modern Toulouse). This posed a threat to the Province. He managed to prevent the Helvetii crossing at Geneva, whereupon they headed for a northern route via the territory of the Aedui, a tribe friendly to Rome, and the Sequani. Caesar pursued them with five legions and some Gallic cavalry under Dumnorix. He managed to bring them to battle: the battle was conclusive as Caesar seized the supplies of the Helvetii and the 130,000 survivors had to surrender. Caesar ordered them to return to their lands as he did not wish a tempting vacuum to be left open to greedy Germans.

The Gauls were greatly impressed by Cae-

sar's success. The tribal chiefs, with Diviciacus, the Chief Druid, as their spokesman,
appealed to Caesar to rid them of the scourge
of Ariovistus. This project met his approval
as German tribes, such as the Cimbri and
Teutoni, frequently irrupted into Gaul,
sometimes travelling as far as Italy. He
approached Ariovistus for a parley, but this
was rejected. He then sent an ultimatum
forbidding Germans to cross the Rhine, to
which Ariovistus replied that he would do as
he pleased. News also arrived that the Suebi,
another German tribe, were gathering and
would be joining Ariovistus. Caesar had to
move fast. He now heard that Ariovistus
intended seizing Vesontio (Besançon),
which was well fortified and supplied; by
forced marches, he beat Ariovistus to it. The
two armies then circled warily around one
another, until Ariovistus began to run out of

POMPEY'S HEAD
shown to Cæsar.

Pompey's head is shown to Caesar

Caesar returns to Rome triumphant

supplies and offered battle. The Romans managed to destroy the left wing of the enemy, but then their own began to fall back. Publius Crassus, Crassus's son, restored the situation and the Germans fled back to the Rhine. A few, including Ariovistus, managed to get across, while the rest were slaughtered by Caesar's cavalry. It was a stunning victory. As soon as the Suebi heard of it, they scurried back to their homes. At the end of 58 BC, Caesar headed off for Cisalpine Gaul to deal with his administrative responsibilities there, and to be in closer touch with events in Rome.

In the north of Gaul, the Belgae, a part-Germanic tribe, were growing alarmed by developments to the south. They feared, with good reason, that they were next in line for being pacified, and had no intention of losing their independence. Accordingly, they prepared for war. As soon as Caesar heard of this, he took two new legions north to Vesontio. After he had ensured his food supply, he quickly moved north to the Marne, the southern border of Belgae territory. There, the Remi, a tribe living round Reims, under the control of another tribe, the Suessiones, sought protection from this unexpected deliverer, and this was granted. The Remi told Caesar that the other Belgic tribes were ready for war and were being joined by Germans from over the Rhine. Galba, king of the Suessiones, was in command of over 300,000 warriors, including 60,000 Bellovaci, 50,000 Suessiones and 50,000 Nervii, the last of whom were actually trained.

The campaign began with much skirmishing

as the Belgae ravaged the lands of the Remi until Caesar drove them off. He also asked Diviciacus to attack the home territory of the Bellovaci, and this threat caused the latter's departure from the Belgic army. The two armies then sat facing each other, separated by a marsh which neither wanted to be first across. Eventually the Belgae withdrew as supplies ran low, promising to gather again to protect any tribe that might come under threat. As soon as Caesar realized their withdrawal was not a ruse, he began to pursue them and seized Noviodunum (Pommiers) from the Suessiones. He then took Bratuspantium from the Bellovaci. Shortly afterwards, Caesar was nearly ambushed successfully by the Nervii, the Atrebates and the Viromandui while setting up camp. Luckily, his men were sufficiently disciplined to resist and Labienus saw what was happening and led his legion, which had been capturing the enemy camp, back into the rear of the Nervii, who were wiped out. Shortly afterwards, the other Belgae surrendered, while Publius Crassus suppressed the tribes on the Atlantic coast.

Caesar returned to Italy where he was voted a fifteen days' thanksgiving, an unprecedented honour.

56 BC opened with bad news. The Veneti, a tribe of skilful seamen, who had a virtual monopoly of trade with Britain, heard that Caesar was contemplating an invasion, which would ruin them. The Britons were also aware of this potential threat and, the previous year, had sent contingents to Gaul to help in the struggle against the Romans. In the previous year, the Veneti had surrendered

hostages to the Romans after their defeat; now they seized Roman corn collectors sent out by Publius Crassus, so as to have something to swap for their own hostages before they went to war. By doing so, they played into Caesar's hands: he knew he would have to completely subjugate them if he wanted control of the Channel and a safe base in northern France and Brittany, and this was a perfect cause for war. He ordered a fleet to be built and set about reducing their towns – no easy task as many were virtually surrounded by sea, and impregnable when the tide was in. Eventually the Veneti took to the sea in about 220 ships. The Romans were initially nonplussed as to how to deal with them – the Veneti's craft were much more seaworthy than the Roman galleys, and too strongly built to be affected by the galleys' rams. But the Veneti did not use archers and their ships were sail-powered. As the galleys were faster, they were able to draw alongside the Veneti's ships and, with a specially developed pole and hook, grapple on to their rigging and, with a bit of strenuous rowing, pull them overboard, rendering the Veneti helpless. When a fortuitous calm fell, the Veneti were totally at their mercy, and their ships succumbed. Without ships, the Veneti had to surrender. Caesar put the Veneti's senate to death, saying that the corn collectors had been ambassadors, and sold the population as slaves.

The following year, 55 BC, two tribes displaced by the Suebi, the Usipetes and the Tencteri, moved into Belgic territory, where they welcomed. This posed a major threat to peace in Gaul and Caesar realized he would have to nip it in the bud. He caught up with the German army and

C. CAESAR. DICT. PERPETVO.

JULIUS CÆSAR,
Founder of ÿ Roman Empire,
was born at Rome, reigned
3 Years, 11 Months, 15 Days,
was kill'd 44 Years before CHRIST.

Julius Caesar, Roman Emperor

The Emperor at recreation

ordered it to return over the Rhine, offering at the same time to settle it in the territory of a friendly tribe, the Ubii. During a day's truce, to give the two German tribes time to discuss the proposal, Caesar's Gallic cavalry, some 5,000 men, were attacked and dispersed by 800 Germans. The following day, a large delegation of German chiefs arrived at Caesar's camp to apologise for breaking the truce. Caesar immediately seized the lot of them, and rushed out with his troops to the German camp, eight miles away. The German warriors were astonished to see them and, leaderless, panicked. The legionaries slaughtered all whom they found in the camp – the Germans had not even taken up arms – while the cavalry pursued the women and children who had managed to escape. They did not get far, for they soon reached the point where the Meuse joins the

Rhine, which was impassable. Those not already cut down were to drown in the river. Caesar followed this up by building a bridge over the Rhine and devastating the lands of the Sugambri, who had given shelter to the Usipetes' and Tencteri's cavalry.

Despite the lateness of the campaigning season, Caesar decided he still had time to invade Britain, and set of at the end of August, landing between Walmer and Deal. The Britons resisted the landings unsuccessfully, but Caesar did not have the time or the men to properly subdue them. He took some hostages after besting the Britons in several minor battles, but in mid-September decided to return to Gaul before the weather got worse. He then returned to Italy, having ordered the building of a fleet of special transports that could be loaded and beached more easily (several unbeached ships had been destroyed in a gale the previous summer) and more galleys. In the spring of 54 BC he returned to Portus Itius (Wissant) where he ordered the Gallic chieftains to present themselves, which they duly did; he then took them hostage, apart from Dumnorix, who escaped, but was pursued and killed. He then set out with 800 ships for Britain. The size of the fleet completely terrified the Britons and they fled inland. But defeating them was not as easy as expected, because their leader, Cassivellaunus, was extremely resourceful, resorting to guerrilla warfare. Caesar eventually wore him down, and he surrendered, promising hostages and tribute. The promises were worthless, being unenforceable, the minute Caesar left British shores.

While Caesar had been away in Britain, the
Gallic chieftains began to plot how to throw
out the Romans. Caesar's legionary camps
were scattered in the territory of the Belgae,
unable to come to each other's aid quickly.
Ambiorix, chief of the Eburones, exploited
this and managed to lure out and ambush the
garrison of one, virtually wiping it out. The
Nervii and the Aduataci were inspired by
Ambiorix's success and laid siege to one of
the other camps – they had learned well from
their Roman conquerors the art of siegecraft.
Caesar managed to drive off this assault. He
then attempted to pursue Ambiorix, but the
latter always managed to evade him, fleeing
to the German forests which were too
dangerous for the legionaries. Caesar managed to destroy the crops and homes of the
Eburones and had one rebel leader flogged to
death, but he did not end the revolt.

It blew up again the following year, when Roman corn-traders were massacred in Cenabum (Orleans) by the chiefs of the Carnutes, Cotuatus and Conconnetodumnus. Within hours, the news was relayed to Vercingetorix, a chief of the Arverni. He immediately set about preparing for war, rousing the other tribes, some of whom he sent to attack the Ruteni, a tribe just outside the Province. Caesar was cut off from his legions as he had been in Italy, but managed to traverse the snow-bound Cevennes, and put together a makeshift army which he led to the territory of the Arverni (now, in turn, cut off to the south). The Arverni now called off the attack on the Ruteni and moved north. But Caesar was ahead of them and managed to surprise and sack Orleans. He then besieged Avaricum (Bourges), the capital of the Bituriges, allies of Vercingetorix.

After a hard-fought siege, the town was taken and its population massacred. The Gauls had practised a scorched-earth policy to impede the Roman advance, but, because of the capture of Avaricum, Caesar was able to replenish his supplies and pursue Vercingetorix to his capital, Gergovia. Gergovia was sited on a 1,200 foot hilltop; the town was walled and the hill steeply sloped, and Caesar was unable to capture it and had to withdraw. Vercingetorix then assembled the Gallic chieftains and was elected supreme commander. He decided to move to Alesia (Mount Auxois) to gather his forces. Caesar pursued him there and built 25 miles of earthworks to hem Vercingetorix in. A relieving army was unable to dislodge the Romans and eventually the gauls were beaten. In their flight, they were slaughtered in large numbers. Vercingetorix sur-

Caesar is assassinated in the Senate

Public grieving at Caesar's funeral

rendered to Caesar. Caesar imposed the relatively light tribute of 40 million sesterces on the Gauls. He also allowed the Gauls to retain their existing forms of government, and released many prisoners: his clemency was motivated by the idea of winning the Gauls' loyalty. Apart from mopping up, the revolt was at an end.

THE CIVIL WAR

While Caesar had been in Gaul, events in Rome had led to a resurgence of chaos. Pompey and Crassus were unwilling allies, and neither had the military forces to control the city. Consequently, the city was under the sway of Publius Clodius and Titus Annius Milo, with their 'Blue' and 'Green' factions, respectively supporters of Caesar and Pompey. In 57 BC a new consul, Lentulus Spinther, proposed Cicero's recall. With the support of Pompey, Cicero returned. Cicero proposed that Pompey be given control of Rome's corn supply and an army and fleet to secure this. He also tried to break up the triumvirate by advocating that Caesar's laws be repealed. But Pompey and Crassus knew how powerful the triumvirate was as a group and met Caesar at Luca, where they agreed that Pompey and Crassus should be consuls for 55 BC and thereafter be assigned the important provinces of Spain and Syria. Caesar's governorship of Gaul was to be extended by five years. Not surprisingly, when Cicero heard this news, he tacked around and proposed a thanksgiving service for Caesar's victories.

Crassus and Pompey ensured that the measures confirming the triumvirate's decisions were enacted through a mixture of violence and bribery. Even so, the consuls elected were Domitius Ahenobarbus and Appius Claudius, opponents of the two leading triumvirs.

In November 54 BC, Crassus left for Syria. In May 53 BC he was defeated at Carrhae, the worst defeat for the Roman army since Cannae (against Hannibal), and killed. This ended the triumvirate. Also Pompey's wife, Julia, Caesar's sister, had died, thus snapping the family bond between the two men.

In Rome, political violence continued: Clodius was murdered by Milo in a brawl, the Senate was burned to the ground and senators were struck down. To restore order, Pompey was elected sole consul. Caesar was in a difficult position. If he wished to become a consul he would first have to become a private citizen again, and this would expose

The ruins of the Colosseum in modern Rome

Shakespeare's dramatization of Julius Caesar

him to prosecution for acts he had committed during his first consulship. The Senate was also agitating for successors to be appointed to Caesar's governorships. This would lead to him being without an army and put him in a very weak position. To prevent this, he bribed Gaius Scribonius Curio to veto any hostile legislation being passed. His faction was not strong enough, though, to prolong his governorships. Finally, when Curio's tribuneship was about to expire, Caesar sent an ultimatum to the consuls, Lucius Cornelius Lentulus and Gaius Claudius Marcellus, that he would return if Pompey were to disband his troops at the same time as he did. Caesar also ensured that Mark Antony and Quintus Cassius, two supporters, were elected tribunes, through bribery. Mark Antony and Cassius were thrown out of the Senate and fled to join Caesar in Ravenna. The Senate then proscribed Caesar. They thought he would await the arrival of his legions stationed in Gaul, but Caesar was always one for striking hard and fast.

Caesar gave the order to march, ordering his men to occupy Ariminum (Rimini). *En route* was the Rubicon, the border between Cisalpine Gaul, his territory, and Roman Italy. Apparently he stopped at the stream, lost in thought. He is reported to have said, 'Comrades, if I stop here, it will be the beginning of my sorrows; if I cross over, it will be such for all mankind.' Civil war was an appalling thought. He began to cross on 10 January 50 BC.

Pompey had more legions but Caesar had more prestige, with his recent conquest of

Gaul. He also understood that in a civil war it is vital to win the support of the populace. This would help him gain the upper hand and also demoralize enemy troops, who could provide a rich recruiting ground, especially if their cause was not clearly winning.

In the event, Pompey abandoned Rome, knowing that he could still count on the support of his legions in Spain, Macedonia and the East, but not on that of his legions in Italy. Rome was thrown into uproar and panic on Caesar's approach. Caesar ignored Rome as he wanted to bring Pompey to battle before he could escape to Macedonia. He spared the leaders of Pompeian garrisons, even allowing them to keep their property, and his invasion was almost bloodless. He just failed to trap Pompey in Brundisium

(Brindisi). Returning to Rome, he reassured the Senate of his good intentions and prepared to pursue the war abroad. In Spain, he managed to surround the Pompeian army and cause its surrender almost without any bloodshed. He then disbanded it, and returned to Rome, where he had been made dictator in his absence. As this was unconstitutional, Caesar had himself elected consul and settled affairs in Rome for the coming year.

Caesar then pursued Pompey over the Adriatic. Pompey did not expect Caesar to cross at this stage. Caesar's admiral, C. Cornelius Dolabella, had been defeated by Scribonius Libo and Marcus Octavius, and the remains of his fleet were no match for Pompey's. The bold step was to sail, even though he was virtually unprotected, so as to surprise his enemy and this step Caesar took. He then laid siege to Pompey in Dyrrachium (Durres, Albania) on the coast, so as to deprive him of an important naval base and open up the Adriatic to his troop transports. As Pompey had command of the sea, he was able to circumvent Caesar's work and gain access to supplies. An inconclusive battle was fought: Caesar's troops were routed, but luckily Pompey did not pursue. Labienus, a lieutenant of Pompey's, killed all the prisoners.

Caesar's army managed to escape successfully and, more by luck than judgement, met up with Domitius Calvinus, who had been dispatched with two legions to contain Metellus Scipio in Macedonia. Pompey marched to Scipio's aid, apparently with the aim of waging a war of attrition against

Caesar, but he was persuaded to seek battle. At Pharsalus (Fersala, Greece) the two armies met. Pompey's was riven with disputes over how to divide the spoils of victory, whereas Caesar's was refreshed, having retreated to the fertile fields of Thessaly. Caesar had 22,000 men, Pompey 45,000. Pompey tried to outflank the right wing of Caesar's army with his cavalry, but Caesar spotted this ploy and hid six cohorts of infantry behind his own cavalry. When Pompey's cavalry charged, they broke on the ranks of infantry and, in their retreat, disordered and abandoned their supporting light infantry, who fled in panic. The six cohorts then turned in on Pompey's line, already engaged with Caesar's, and put it to flight. The battle was effectively over.

Pompey went to Egypt and requested the

king, Ptolemy XIII, to protect him. Ptolemy was at war with his sister, Cleopatra VII. By a ruse, Ptolemy lured Pompey ashore and had him murdered and beheaded. When Caesar arrived, Ptolemy had the head presented to him. According to Plutarch, Caesar was disgusted and wept.

Instead of returning to Italy and ending the Civil War, Caesar now decided, rather quixotically, to sort out the Egyptian Civil War. This episode lasted eight months, longer than the conquest of Italy and Spain, or the campaign in Greece.

Caesar's absence from Italy was leading to a resurgence of unrest and a decline in authority. Elsewhere, Pharnaces, son of Mithridates the Great, had overrun Armenia Minor and Cappadocia. The two states appealed for help and Domitius Calvinus, now stationed in Pontus, responded. Pharnaces defeated the Romans and their allies, and Caesar rushed to Pontus to stop the rot. At the Battle of Zela (Zilleh, Turkey), Caesar destroyed Pharnaces's army, and uttered the immortal words, '*Veni, vidi, vici*'.

Caesar was now supreme in the Roman world.

A GOD ON EARTH

On landing at Tarentum (Taranto, Italy) in
September 47 BC, Caesar found he had been
elected dictator for the second time. Back in
Rome, he restored the Senate to its normal
size, and placated those who were expecting
to be rewarded at the expense of the Pompeians. Discipline in the army was collapsing,
as his soldiers had not been paid their prize
money or discharged. Eventually they camped outside Rome, where Caesar shamed
them into line, by addressing them as citi-

zens, not soldiers. He needed them for his next campaign in Africa, where Cato, Scipio, Pompey's two sons, Gnaeus and Sextus, and others, had raised the Pompeian standard. The delay in sorting out problems in Rome had allowed them to accumulate a considerable force – ten legions – allied to the four legions of King Juba of Numidia (Algeria). They had laid in stores and fortified the towns.

Fortunately for Caesar, they had also alienated the local population by seizing goods, and King Juba had angered Bocchus and Bogud, the kings of Mauritania (Morocco). Scipio also ignored Cato's wise advice to wear Caesar down by endless marching, rather than face him in battle with his untested recruits. Even so, at one battle, Labienus nearly succeeded in destroying Caesar's army, and it is not clear how Caesar escaped. Caesar retired to Ruspina (Monastir, Tunisia), fortified it and sent for reinforcements. Scipio and Labienus camped outside, awaiting the arrival of Juba. Supplies ran low in Ruspina, and Caesar became more and more impatient of rescue. At the end of January 46 BC, a corn fleet arrived, followed by a troop convoy ferrying two legions from Sicily. Juba aborted his attempt to link up with the Pompeians, as Bocchus had taken advantage of his absence to destroy and plunder the richest town in Numidia. Two more legions arrived shortly after. Caesar decided to break out of Ruspina. Near Thapsus (between Sfax and Sousse in Tunisia) the two armies collided. Scipio had been rejoined by Juba with his Numidian cavalry and elephants. After a few days' manoeuvring, the armies drew up in lines of battle. For some reason, Scipio's front line did not organize itself in a disciplined way. Caesar's troops could not restrain themselves: they rushed forwards, against orders. Caesar's archers and slingers assaulted the elephants, which were terrified, wheeling round and trampling on their own troops. The Numidian cavalry panicked, and, within minutes, Scipio's army had become a terrified, fleeing rabble. Caesar's troops, beside themselves with blood-lust, pursued and massacred them. For the loss of about 50 Caesarians, 10,000 Pompeians are said to have died. The Pompeian generals escaped only to perish shortly thereafter, with only Labienus living to fight another day.

On his return to Rome, Caesar promised clemency, and proceeded to lay on extraordinary and lavish games. His power was absolute.

Trouble now broke out in Spain, where Gnaeus and Sextus Pompey commanded several legions. Caesar travelled there as quickly as possible and eventually brought them to battle at Munda (site unknown), and after a particularly hard-fought struggle, prevailed. Labienus was finally killed and, shortly afterwards, Gnaeus Pompey was hunted down and beheaded. All opposition was at an end.

After Munda, Caesar received a fifty days' thanksgiving and received the title of imperator (supreme commander) for life. He was deified and elected consul for ten years. He shared power with no one, needing no one's support. He was incredibly rich from the spoils of his campaigns, so he could bribe anybody and everybody, and he had a loyal army behind him. He enlarged the Senate from 600 to 900, and packed it with his supporters, including Gauls, which caused great resentment. He gave Latin rights to Spain, Sicily and Gaul, and reformed the tax system in the East, so that it would not be too oppressive. He ordered the establishment of colonies to settle his veterans. His plans were equally monumental: the rebuilding of Carthage and Corinth, the defeat of the Parthians, and the construction of vast municipal buildings and temples in Rome itself. He had also drawn up his will, leaving his estate to his great-nephew Gaius Octavius Thurinus, who adopted the name Gaius Julius Caesar Octavianus, later to be Augustus.

A craven Senate fuelled his vanity by naming him *Pater Patriae* (Father of the Country), and putting his head on coins, usually a monarch's right. He was declared a god.

They renamed the month of *Quintilis* (the fifth month), *Julius* (July). The title of king was offered to him at the *Lupercalia*, a festival in honour of Pan, but apparently he rejected it when the crowd did not seem to approve. The other side of all this flattery was the growth of a conspiracy, probably led by Cassius, and involving Marcus Brutus, two forgiven Pompeians, and about sixty others. The pretext for the conspiracy was tyrannicide. In fact, they probably wanted to restore the Senate to its previous power.

On the ides of March (15th), Caesar set out for the Senate. He was probably aware of the conspiracy, but relied on the senators' oath to protect him. Antony was detained at the entrance to the Senate and Decimus Brutus had placed some gladiators in the Theatre of Pompey in case Caesar was too well protected. Caesar entered the Senate and sat in the gilded regal chair that the senators had awarded him. Tullius Cimber approached him and appealed for the recall of his brother. Caesar refused this. Cimber grabbed his purple toga and exposed Caesar's neck. At this signal, C. Servilius Casca rushed forward and tried to stab Caesar in the throat, but missed, causing a minor wound in the neck. Cimber grabbed Caesar's hand but Caesar leapt forward and hurled Casca to the ground. The other murderers closed in while the senators watched, aghast. Caesar was stabbed twenty-three times.

Suetonius declares that, because of failing health, Caesar had no particular desire to prolong his life. His only fear was that his untimely death would lead to a civil war worse than that he had won.

LIFE AND TIMES

Julius Caesar
Hitler
Monet
Van Gogh
Beethoven
Mozart
Mother Teresa
Florence Nightingale
Anne Frank
Napoleon

LIFE AND TIMES

FURTHER MINI SERIES
INCLUDE

ILLUSTRATED POETS

Robert Burns
Shakespeare
Oscar Wilde
Emily Dickinson
Christina Rossetti
Shakespeare's Love Sonnets

FURTHER MINI SERIES INCLUDE

HEROES OF THE WILD WEST

General Custer
Butch Cassidy and the Sundance Kid
Billy the Kid
Annie Oakley
Buffalo Bill
Geronimo
Wyatt Earp
Doc Holliday
Sitting Bull
Jesse James